LIBER SPIRITUM

LIBER
SPIRITUM

BY ARUNDELL OVERMAN

Copyright 2020 by Arundell Overman

ISBN: 9798698992417

CONTENTS

INTRODUCTION
7

THE 144 SPIRITS LISTED IN ALPHABETICAL ORDER
11

INTRODUCTION

ALL the spirits in this book were once gods and demons of various cultures around the world. As such, from the perspective of the Witch, or Demonolater, they are real beings, that exist within the ocean of energy that surrounds our planet earth. It is important to note that this book forms a Pantheon, a system of "many gods." As such, each one of these spirits can be invoked for various reasons. What are these reasons? The same reasons that the ancient people had when they invoked their gods. For luck, for wisdom, for healing, for spell casting, for help with love, lust, illness, destruction, change in the weather, etc. Success in the work depends on your power to call them, and their power to answer. Spirits are not all knowing.

Spirits are not all good, or all bad. Like humans, their nature is mixed good and bad. They have their limits, yet they can do amazing things, and one can contact them face to face, as one might talk to a human, yet they are made from the astral light. I came face to face with several of the spirits in this book, starting with Asmodeus, and that is why I have taken the time to compile it.

There are many different methods of invoking gods and demons to visible appearance, and many books written on how to call them with various magic ceremonies and rituals. In the age we now live in one can easily find hundreds of these, yet many of them contain information that is useless at best. It is not the purpose of this book to outline a new method of calling spirits, or a set of exercises which you must follow. Rather, my aim is to present the list of demons, gods, goddesses, and spirits, and to explain a set of principles by which, you may craft your own method of working with these spirits, should you choose to do so. Those already familiar with the process of invoking spirits may simply incorporate these spirits into their own practice, or already existing magical system.

The lesser key of Solomon: Goetia, The Grand Grimoire, the Red Dragon, the Black Dragon, The Grimoire of Pope Honorius, The Grimorium Verum, the Infernal Dictionary, and several other books have been the sources for this text, and there are in addition, a few very important spirits from the Pantheons around the world, the source of each spirit being named. Each spirit is carefully listed by its description in the original source material it comes from first, and then any other source material is listed, and then finally, my own notes added at the end of the description of the spirit. In this way, if you like, you may do further research on these spirits, and follow them back in history as far as you can.

Let us consider for a moment the word Demonolatry. It means the worship of demons. But what does this mean? What are the demons? Why would someone worship them, and what does it mean to worship? First, let us define the word demon. Daemon is the original Greek, and it did not mean evil spirit, it simply meant spirit, or Genius. Socrates had a Daemon, and it was considered his instructor, what we might call a spirit guide. After the word was picked up and used in the New Testament of the Christian bible, it came to mean exclusively an evil spirit, and one in the service of the king of all evil spirits, the Devil.

As time went on, and Christianity grew older, ALL gods, goddesses, and spirits of all kinds, including fairies, kelpies, elves, and any other sort of pagan spirit was classified as a demon in Christian mythology. They simply had no other place to put them, as anything that was not a part of the traditional dogma and authority of the church was looked at as being pagan, and thus, demonic. The justification for this was spelled out in the bible in verses such as 1 Corinthians 10:20 where Saint Paul writes "No, but the sacrifices of pagans are offered to demons, not to God, and I do not want you to be participants with demons." Who do the pagans sacrifice to? Their gods, which the bible clearly labels as DEMONS.

To make his point especially clear, Paul continues in the next verse. "You cannot drink the cup of the Lord, and the cup of demons too, you cannot partake from the table of the Lord and the table of demons too." And then in the next verse: "Are we trying to provoke the lord to jealousy? Are we stronger than he?" So, you can see that by these verses, ALL gods, goddesses, and pagan spirits have been transformed into demons by the words given in the Bible.

These verses shaped the worldview of the coming ages, yet the spirits themselves were not lost to mankind. They remained as the demons of the new religion, and heretics and witches continued to invoke them, though in the end, it became a crime punishable by death. It has been said "the old gods did not die; they fell into hell and became devils."

So, we can see that in this book there is a mix of many different spirits. How would a person go about contacting, working with, or invoking one of these spirits? First realize that doing so is not a thing to be taken lightly. Many of these spirits are dangerous. To invoke or call upon any one of them is to take a step down the road of witchcraft, and sorcery. And you can't know the end of the journey upon the first step!

The first key to invoking the spirit is its image. All ancient gods and spirits had an idol, and it was before their idol that offerings were made, in expectation of service and protection, etc, from the god or spirit. The idol of that god was often placed in a special shrine, or temple, and small gifts were left before it in offering. This is the idolatry so heavily condemned in the Christian bible. So, therefore, the practice is up to you, you have an image, you can paint it, draw it, carve it, print it off and glue it to the wall, in a corner, a room, an empty building, or a temple made of stone.

The next thing is to make the spirit an offering, some kind of gift, to honor it, to make it a tiny part of your life, to share with it, your energy, or to give it something you think it might like. A coin, a candle, a bit of incense, a flower, whiskey, blood, etc. You can also get clues about what the spirit might like from the descriptions of the spirits listed in the book. Remember no book is infallible, and the book these illustrations is taken from is no exception. If you decide to work with one of the spirits, you can also do research on it in as many places as possible, to learn as much about it as you can.

Using that knowledge alone can take you as far as the ancients, because if you make real contact with the spirit, it will begin to communicate to you in various ways. You may see it directly made of energy, moving around your house. You may feel an unmistakable presence in the room where the shrine is or experience other phenomena such as seeing light come out of the picture of the spirit, or seeing the picture move as if alive. If you are sensitive to energy, or if one of these spirits has already chosen you and is attempting to make contact with you through this book, you may perceive that this book itself is "haunted" or glows, or talks, etc. It is a book of spirits, and with these instructions, a grimoire even.

Therefore, I leave you with these simple things to consider. If you choose to contact one of the spirits of the book, you may do so simply by following the principles I described. An image, a description of the spirit to be called, a small shrine or area to place the image of the spirit, perhaps a candle or a bit of incense there...can you see it in the eye of your mind? Once you have made contact, all you must do is talk, and the spirit will take it from there, I can tell you no more. At that point it is between you and the spirit. With these sayings I wish you well.

-ARUNDELL OVERMAN

ABADDON

ABADDON, the angel of death and destruction. The Hebrew term Abaddon, meaning "doom", and its Greek equivalent Apollyon appear in the Bible as both a place of destruction and an angel of the abyss. In the Hebrew Bible, Abaddon is used with reference to a bottomless pit, often appearing alongside the place Sheol, the realm of the dead.

In the New Testament Book of Revelation, an angel called Abaddon is described as the king of an army of locusts; his name is first transcribed in Greek, in Revelation 9:11—"whose name in Hebrew is Abaddon, The Angel of Death."

NOTES: Text and sigil by Arundell Overman, the full text of Revelation chapter 9 is printed below.

REVELATION CHAPTER 9, KING JAMES VERSION (KJV)

1. And the fifth angel sounded, and I saw a star fall from heaven unto the earth: and to him was given the key of the bottomless pit.

2. And he opened the bottomless pit; and there arose a smoke out of the pit, as the smoke of a great furnace; and the sun and the air were darkened by reason of the smoke of the pit.

3. And there came out of the smoke locusts upon the earth: and unto them was given power, as the scorpions of the earth have power.

4. And it was commanded them that they should not hurt the grass of the earth, neither any green thing, neither any

tree; but only those men which have not the seal of God in their foreheads.

5. And to them it was given that they should not kill them, but that they should be tormented five months: and their torment was as the torment of a scorpion, when he striketh a man.

6. And in those days shall men seek death and shall not find it; and shall desire to die, and death shall flee from them.

7. And the shapes of the locusts were like unto horses prepared unto battle; and on their heads were as it were crowns like gold, and their faces were as the faces of men.

8. And they had hair as the hair of women, and their teeth were as the teeth of lions.

9. And they had breastplates, as it were breastplates of iron; and the sound of their wings was as the sound of chariots of many horses running to battle.

10. And they had tails like unto scorpions, and there were stings in their tails: and their power was to hurt men five months.

11. And they had a king over them, which is the angel of the bottomless pit, whose name in the Hebrew tongue is Abaddon, but in the Greek tongue hath his name Apollyon.

12. One woe is past; and behold, there come two woes more hereafter.

13. And the sixth angel sounded, and I heard a voice from the four horns of the golden altar, which is before God,

14. Saying to the sixth angel which had the trumpet, Loose the four angels which are bound in the great river Euphrates.

15. And the four angels were loosed, which were prepared for an hour, and a day, and a month, and a year, for to slay the third part of men.

16. And the number of the army of the horsemen were two hundred thousand thousand: and I heard the number of them.

17. And thus I saw the horses in the vision, and them that sat on them, having breastplates of fire, and of jacinth, and

brimstone: and the heads of the horses were as the heads of lions; and out of their mouths issued fire and smoke and brimstone.

18. By these three was the third part of men killed, by the fire, and by the smoke, and by the brimstone, which issued out of their mouths.

19. For their power is in their mouth, and in their tails: for their tails were like unto serpents, and had heads, and with them they do hurt.

20. And the rest of the men which were not killed by these plagues yet repented not of the works of their hands, that they should not worship devils, and idols of gold, and silver, and brass, and stone, and of wood: which neither can see, nor hear, nor walk:

21. Neither repented they of their murders, nor of their sorceries, nor of their fornication, nor of their thefts.

ABIGOR

ABIGOR, Eligor. The demon of a higher order, grand Duke in the infernal monarchy. Sixty legions march under his command. He shows himself in the figure of a handsome rider carrying the spear, the standard, or the scepter; He skillfully responds to everything about the secrets of war, knows the future, and teaches the leaders the means to be loved by soldiers.

NOTES: Image and text, Dictionnaire Infernal, Sigil, Lesser Key of Solomon.

ABIGOR

ABRAXAS

ABRACAX or Abraxas, one of the gods of some Asian théogonies, whose name was drawn from the Philactère Abracadabra. Abracax is depicted on amulets with a head-of rooster, dragon feet and a whip in his hand. The demonologists have made him a demon, who has the head of a king and the feet of snakes. The Basilidiens, heretics of the second century, saw in him their supreme god, because they found that the seven Greek letters of which they formed his name, made in Greek letters, the number 365, which is that of the days of the year,. They placed under his orders several geniuses who presided over the three hundred and sixty-five, and to whom they attributed three hundred and sixty-five virtues, one for each day. The Basilidiens said that Jesus Christ, our Lord, was only a benevolent ghost sent to the earth by Abracax. They deviated from the doctrine of their leader.

NOTES: Image and Text, Dictionnaire Infernal. Sigil by Arundell Overman.

ABRAXAS

ADRAMELECH

ADRAMELECH, Grand Chancellor of the underworld, steward of the wardrobe of the sovereign of demons, President of the High Council of the Devils. It was worshipped in Sépharvaïm, city of the Assyrians, who burned children on his altars. The Rabbis say he shows himself under the figure of a mule, and sometimes under a peacock.

NOTES: Image and Text, Dictionnaire Infernal, sigil by Arundell Overman.

ADRAMELECH

AGALIAREPT

AGALIAREPT, who has the power to discover the most hidden secrets, in all the Courts and Governments of the world, he reveals the greatest mysteries. He commands the second legion of spirits, he has under him Buer, Gusoan and Botis.

NOTES: Text and Sigil from the Red Dragon, art created for this book by Artem Grigoryev.

AGALIAREPT

AGLASIS

AGLASIS, who can carry anyone or anything anywhere in the world.

NOTES: Text from the Grimorium Verum. Sigil created by Arundell Overman. Art by Artem Grigoryev.

AGLASIS

AGRAT BAT MAHALAT

AGRAT bat Mahalat. MAHLAT and Agrat are proper names, "bat" meaning "daughter of" (Hebrew). Therefore, Agrat bat Mahlat means "Agrat, daughter of Mahlat."

In the Rabbinic literature of Yalkuṭ Ḥadash, on the eves of Wednesday and Saturday, she is "the dancing roof-demon" who haunts the air with her chariot and her train of 18 messengers/angels of spiritual destruction. She dances while her mother, or possibly grandmother, Lilith howls. She is also "the mistress of the sorceresses" who communicated magic secrets to Amemar, a Jewish sage. In Zoharistic Kabbalah, she is a queen of the demons and an angel of sacred prostitution, who mates with archangel Samael along with Lilith and Naamah, sometimes adding Eisheth as a fourth mate.

NOTES: Sigil and text by Arundell Overman.

AGUARÈS

AGUARÈS, Grand Duke of the eastern part of Hell. He shows himself in the form of a Lord riding on a crocodile, with a hawk on his fist. He brings back the fugitives of the party that he protects and puts the enemy in rout. He gives dignity, teaches all languages, and makes to dance, the spirits of the Earth. This leader of the Demons is of the order of virtues: he has under his laws Thirty-one legions.

NOTES: Text and image from the Dictionnaire Infernal, sigil from the Lesser Key of Solomon.

AGUARÈS

ALASTOR

ALASTOR. Stern demon, supreme executor of the infernal monarch's sentences. He has the function of a Nemesis. Zoroaster calls him the executioner; Origen says it is the same as Azazel. Others confuse it with the Exterminator Angel. The elders called evil spirits Alastores, and Plutarch said that Cicero, out of hatred against Augustus, had the plan of killing himself at the hearth of that Prince to become his Alastor.

NOTES: Text and Image from the Dictionnaire Infernal, Sigil by Arundell Overman.

ALASTOR

ALOCER

ALOCER, Mighty demon, grand Duke in the underworld; He shows himself dressed as a knight, mounted on a huge horse; His figure recalls the traits of the lion; He has the fiery complexion, the fiery eyes; He speaks with gravity; He teaches the secrets of astronomy and liberal arts; He dominates Thirty-six Legions.

NOTES: Text and image from the Dictionnaire Infernal, sigil from the lesser key of Solomon.

ALOCER

AMAYMON

The Spirit Amaymon is great, high, and mighty, and terrible in appearance. He usually assumes the form of an old man, with a long beard, his ears being like those of a horse, with a royal diadem on his head. His first appearance is unusually tremendous; forked lightning and deep mouthed thunders, shaking the earth apparently to the center, announce his awful presence. Then suddenly the earth will appear to vomit forth gushes of flame, and sulfurous odors taint the charmed atmosphere. Anon are heard all sorts of musical instruments, then an uncouth clatter of creaking wheels and horrid crashes will every instant astound the invocator, but on a sudden will all be again calm, and clothed in the whole pomp of his spiritual grandeur, attended by countless legions of invincible spirits. Amaymon will be seen riding furiously upon a fierce and roaring lion. He will approach to the utmost limits of the space assigned him, and it will well become the Theurgist to preserve his wonted calmness: for if he powerfully constrain, and urgently invoke, this furious spirit, he may be brought to the most submissive obedience, He has power to give knowledge, dignity, and great promotion.

NOTE: Text from "The astrologer of the 19th century." Sigil taken from the grimoire called "Fasciculus Rerum Geomanticarum."

AMAYMON

AMDUSCIAS

AMDUSCIAS, Grand Duke in the underworld. He has the form of a unicorn; but when it is evoked, it shows itself under a human figure. He gives concerts, if he is commanded; We hear, without seeing anything, the sound of trumpets and other musical instruments. The trees bow to his voice. He orders twenty-nine legions.

NOTE: Text and image from the Dictionnaire Infernal, sigil from the Lesser Key of Solomon.

AMDUSCIAS

AMON

AMON, or Aamon, great and mighty Marquis of the Infernal Empire. He has the figure of a wolf with a serpent's tail; He vomits flames; When he takes the human form, he has a man's shape, only the body; His head looks like that of an owl and in it's beak are very-tapered canine teeth. This is the strongest of demon princes. He knows the past and the future, and reconciles, when he wants, blurred friends. He commands forty legions. The Egyptians saw in Amon or Amoun their supreme god; They represented him with blue skin, in a rather human form.

NOTE: Text and image from the Dictionnaire Infernal, sigil from the Lesser Key of Solomon.

AMON

AMY

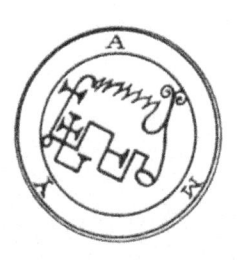

AMY, or Avnas. The Fifty-eighth Spirit is Amy, or Avnas. He is a Great President, and appeareth at first in the Form of a Flaming Fire; but after a while he putteth on the Shape of a Man. His office is to make one Wonderful Knowing[25] in Astrology and all the Liberal Sciences. He giveth Good Familiars and can bewray Treasure that is kept by Spirits. He governeth 36 Legions of Spirits, and his Seal is this, etc.

NOTES: Sigil and text from the Lesser Key of Solomon. Image drawn for this book by Ville Vuorinen.

AMY

ANDRAS

ANDRAS, Grand Marquis in the underworld. We see it appear with the body of an angel, the head of a cat-haunt, (screech owl) straddling a black wolf and bearing in hand a sharp saber. He teaches to those he promotes, how to kill their enemies, masters, and servants. This is he who raises discords and quarrels. He commands thirty legions.

NOTES: Text and image from the Dictionnaire Infernal, sigil from the Lesser Key of Solomon.

ANDRAS

ANDREALPHUS

ANDREALPHUS. The Sixty-fifth Spirit is Andrealphus. He is a Mighty Marquis, appearing at first in the form of a Peacock, with great Noises. But after a time, he putteth on Human shape. He can teach Geometry perfectly. He maketh Men very subtle therein; and in all Things pertaining unto Mensuration or Astronomy. He can transform a Man into the Likeness of a Bird. He governeth 30 Legions of Infernal Spirits, and his Seal is this, etc.

NOTES: Sigil and text from the Lesser Key of Solomon, image, public domain.

ANDREALPHUS

ANDROMALIUS

ANDROMALIUS. The Seventy-second Spirit in (the) Order (of Solomon) is named Andromalius. He is an Earl, Great and Mighty, appearing in the Form of a Man holding a Great Serpent in his Hand. His Office is to bring back both a Thief, and the Goods which be stolen; and to discover all Wickedness, and Underhand Dealing; and to punish all Thieves and other Wicked People and also to discover Treasures that be Hid. He ruleth over 36 Legions of Spirits. His Seal is this, the which wear thou as aforesaid, etc.

NOTES: Text and Sigil from the Lesser key of Solomon, art by Matti Sinkkonen.

ANDROMALIUS

ASMODEUS

ASMODEUS, destruction daemon, the same as Samael, according to some rabbis. He's a superintendent of gambling houses. He sows dissipation and error. — The rabbis say that he once dethroned Solomon; But that soon Solomon charged him with Irons and forced him to help him build the Temple of Jerusalem. — Tobie, following the same rabbis, having driven him away, with the smoke of the spleen of a fish, from the body of the young Sara he possessed. (For Asmodeus loved Sarah) The Angel Raphael was said to have imprisoned Asmodeus at the extremities of Egypt. Paul Lucas says he saw him in one of his travels. He was amused about it; However, it was possible to read in the "Mail from Egypt" that the people of this country still adore the Asmodeus serpent, which has a temple in the desert of Ryanneh. It is added that this snake cuts itself in pieces, and a moment later, it disappears. Asmodeus is, at the judgment of Virsions, the ancient serpent that seduced Eve. The Jews, who call him Asmodai, made him the Prince of Demons, As seen in paraphrase Chaldaïque. It is, in the underworld, as described by Wierus, a strong and powerful king, who has three heads: the first resembles that of a bull, the second to that of a man, the third to that of a ram. He's got a snake tail, goose feet, and fiery breath. He shows himself riding on a dragon, carrying a standard and a spear. He is subjected, however, by the infernal hierarchy, to King Amoymon. When you exorcise him, you have to be firm on your feet, and call him by name. He gives rings made under the influence of a certain constellation; He teaches men to make themselves invisible and also, geometry, arithmetic, astronomy, and mechanical arts. He also knows treasures, which he can be forced to discover; Seventy-two Legions obey him. He is also called Chammadaï and Sydonaï. Asmodeus was one of the demons that possessed Madeleine Bavent. Le Sage made Asmodeus the hero of one of his novels (The Lame Devil).

NOTES: Text and image from the Dictionnaire Infernal, sigil from the Lesser Key of Solomon.

ASMODEUS

ASTAROTH

ASTAROTH, great-Mighty Duke in the underworld. He has the figure of a very ugly angel and shows himself straddling an infernal dragon; He holds in his left hand a viper. Some magicians say that he presides over the West, that he provides the friendship of the Great Lords, and that he must be evoked on Wednesday. The Sidonians and the Philistines adored him. He is said to be the great treasurer in Hell. Wierus teaches us that he knows the past and the future, and that he would be happy to answer questions that we ask to him on the most secret things. It is easy to cause him to talk about the creation and, the faults and the fall of the Angels, about which he knows the whole story. But in his conversations, he argues that for him he was punished unjustly. He teaches liberal arts in depth, and commands forty legions. He who invokes this spirit must be careful to let himself be approached, because of his unbearable stench. That is why it is prudent for the magician to hold under his nostrils a magic ring, made of silver, which is a protection against the evil odors of demons. Astaroth has been present in several possessions. He is quoted as one of the seven princes of hell who visited Faust, according to the English tradition; He appeared as a snake with a colorful tail like changing bricks, two short feet, all yellow, white and yellowish belly, reddish brown neck, and arrow points, like those of the hedgehog, as long as the length of a finger.

NOTES: Text and image from the Dictionnaire Infernal, sigil from the Lesser Key of Solomon.

ASTAROTH

AZAZEL

AZAZEL, second order demon, keeper of the goat. At the Feast of Atonement, which the Jews celebrated on the tenth day of the seventh month, two goats were brought to the high Priest, drawn by fate. (or by drawing lots) One for the Lord, the other for Azazel. The one on whom the fate of the Lord fell was slain, and the blood was used for atonement. The high priest then put his two hands on the head of the other, confessed his sins and those of the people, to lay their burden on this animal, which was then driven into the wilderness and set free. And the people, having left the goat of Azazel, also called the scapegoat, the care of their iniquities, returned in silence.
— According to Milton, Azazel is the first ensign of the Infernal armies. It is also the name of the demon who serves the heretic mark, for his honors.

NOTES: Image and text from the Dictionnaire Infernal. Public domain.

AZAZEL

BAËL

BAËL, Demon quoted in the Grand Grimoire, at the head of the infernal powers. It is by him that Wiérus begins the inventory of his famous Pseudomonarchia Dœmonum. He calls Baël the first king of Hell; His estates are in the eastern part. He shows himself with three heads, one of which has the figure of a toad, the other one of a man, the third one of a cat. His voice is hoarse, but he fights very well. He makes those who invoke him fine and cunning and teaches them the way to be invisible if necessary. Sixty-six legions obeyed him.

NOTES: Image and text from the Dictionnaire Infernal, sigil from the Lesser key of Solomon.

BAËL

BALAN

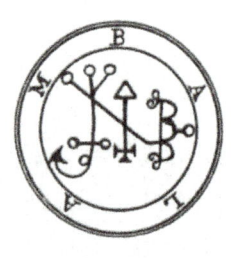

BALAN, great and Terrible king in the Underworld. He sometimes has three heads: that of a bull, that of a man, that of a ram. Join this with a snake tail and eyes that throw out flame. But more ordinarily he shows himself horned, naked and, riding on a bear. He carries a hawk on his fist. His voice is hoarse and violent. He advises on the past, the present and the future. — This demon, who was once of the order of Dominions, and who now commands forty legions of Hell, teaches cunning, finesse and the convenient way to see without being seen.

NOTES: Image and text from the Dictionnaire Infernal, sigil from the lesser key of Solomon.

BALAN

BARBATOS

BARBATOS, Demon, great and mighty, Count Duke in the Underworld, Robin hood type; (similar to Robin of the woods, or Jack in the green) He shows himself under the figure of an archer or a hunter; We meet him in the woods. Four kings sound the horn in front of him. He teaches divination by the singing of the birds, the roar of the bulls, the barking of the dogs and the cries of the various animals. He knows the treasures buried by the magicians. He reconciles blurred friends. This demon, which once was of the order of the virtues of the heavens or that of the dominions, is now reduced to command thirty infernal Legions. He knows the past and the future.

NOTES: Image and text from the Dictionnaire Infernal, sigil from the lesser key of Solomon.

BARBATOS

BATHIN

BATHIN. The Eighteenth Spirit (of the lesser key of Solomon) is Bathin. He is a Mighty and Strong Duke, and appeareth like a Strong Man with the tail of a Serpent, sitting upon a Pale-Coloured Horse. He knoweth the Virtues of Herbs and Precious Stones and can transport men suddenly from one country to another. He ruleth over 30 Legions of Spirits. His Seal is this which is to be worn as aforesaid.

NOTES: Text and Sigil from the Lesser Key of Solomon. Art by Matti Sinkonen.

BATHIN

BECHARD

BECHARD is a demon described in the Keys of Solomon as having power over winds and storms. He causes hail, storms and rain, by means of a malefic curse that he composes with stewed toads and other drugs. (Translated from the French by Aaman Lamba from the Dictionnaire Infernal.)

NOTES: Text from the Dictionnaire Infernal, Sigil from the "Secrets of Solomon." Image public domain, a toad.

BEELZEBUB

BEELZEBUB or Belzebub or Beelzebuth. Prince of Demons, according to the scriptures; The first in power and in crime after Satan. According to Milton; Supreme leader of the Infernal Empire, according to most démonographers. — His name means Lord of the Flies. Bodin claims that he is no longer seen in his temple. It was the Demon most revered of the peoples of Canaan, who sometimes represented him under the figure of a fly, most often with the attributes of the sovereign power. He made Oracles, and King Ochozias consulted him on a sickness which worried him and was severely reprimanded for this by the prophet Elisha. He was given the power to deliver the men from the flies that ruined the harvest. Almost all the démonomanes look at him as the ruler of the Dark Empire, and each one portrays him according to his imagination.

Milton gives him an imposing appearance, and a high wisdom breathes on his face. One says he is as high as a tower; The other of a size equal to ours; Some of them describe him in the form of a snake with the traits of a woman. The monarch of the underworld, says Palingène, in Zodiaco Vitœ, is of a prodigious size, seated on an immense throne, surrounded by a ring of fire, swollen chest, puffy face, gleaming eyes, raised eyebrows and menacing air. It has extremely wide nostrils, and two large horns on the head; He is black as a moor: two broad wings of bats are attached to his shoulders; It has two broad duck legs, a lion's tail, and long hairs from the head to the feet. Some say that Beelzebub is still Priapus; Others, like Porphyry, confuse him with Bacchus. It was thought to be found in the Belbog or Belbach (white God) of the Slavons, because his bloody image was always covered with flies, like that of Beelzebub among the Syrians. It is also said to be the same as Pluto. It is more likely to believe that it is Baël, the demon that Wiérus made emperor of the underworld. All the better that Beelzebub does not appear under his name in the inventory of the Infernal monarchy.

NOTES: Image and text from the Dictionnaire Infernal, sigil from the Grand Grimoire.

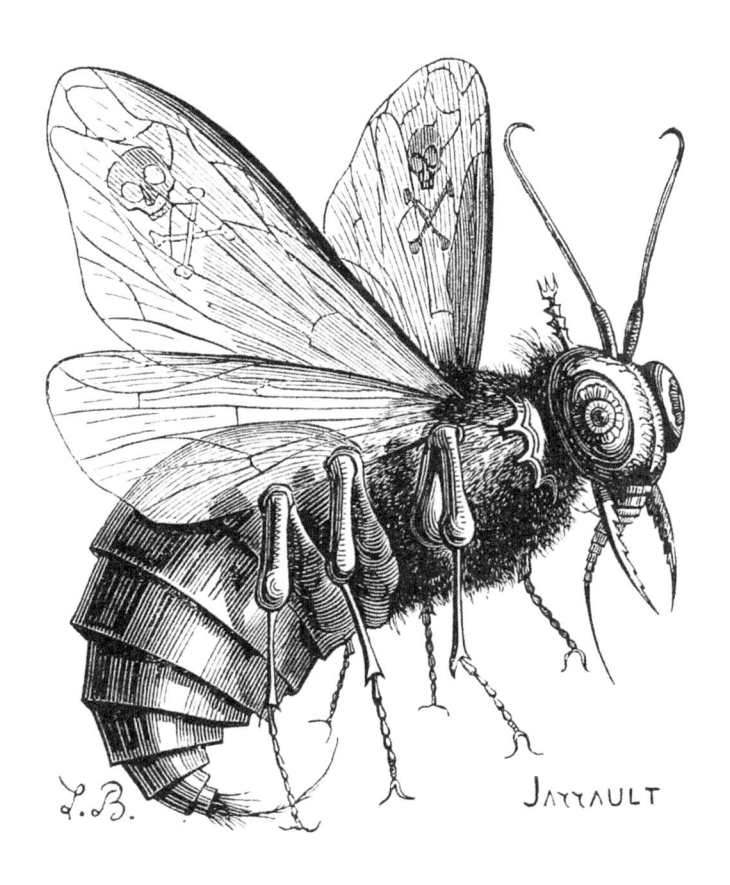

BEELZEBUB

BEHEMOTH

BEHEMOTH, heavy and stupid demon, despite his dignity. His strength is in his loins; His domain is gluttony and the pleasures of the belly. Some démonomanes say he is in the underworld, the cupbearer and Grand Butler. Bodin believes that behemoth is none other than the Pharaoh of Egypt who persecuted the Hebrews. It is spoken of behemoth in Job as a monstrous creature. Commentators claim that it is the whale, and others that it is the elephant; But there were other monsters whose races disappeared. It is seen in the trial of Urbain grander that behemoth is indeed a demon. De Lancer says he was taken for a monstrous animal, because he gives himself the shape of all the big beasts. He adds that behemoth also disguises himself with perfection in dog, Elephant, Fox and Wolf. If Wierus, our Oracle with regard to the demons, does not admit behemoth in his inventory of the infernal monarchy, he says, in his book, "The prestige of the Demons", chapter X that Behemoth or the elephant, could well be Satan himself, which is thus called the vast power. Finally, because one reads, in chapter XL of Job that behemoth eats hay like an ox, the rabbis made him the wonderful ox reserved for the feast of their Messiah. This ox is so huge, they say, that he swallows every day the hay of a thousand immense mountains, which he has grazed since the beginning of the world. He never leaves his thousand mountains, where the grass he ate during the day regrows during the night. They add that God killed the female of this ox in the beginning; For we could not allow such a breed to multiply. The Jews promise well of joy at the feast where he will make the piece of resistance. (piece de resistance) They swear on their side, by the flesh of Behemoth.

NOTES: Image and text from the Dictionnaire Infernal. Sigil by Arundell Overman.

BEHEMOTH

BELIAL

BELIAL. The Sixty-eighth Spirit is Belial. He is a Mighty and a Powerful King and was created next after LUCIFER. He appeareth in the Form of Two Beautiful Angels sitting in a Chariot of Fire. He speaketh with a Comely Voice, and declareth that he fell first from among the worthier sort, that were before Michael, and other Heavenly Angels. His Office is to distribute Presentations and Senatorships, etc.; and to cause favour of Friends and of Foes. He giveth excellent Familiars, and governeth 50 Legions of Spirits. Note well that this King Belial must have Offerings, Sacrifices and Gifts presented unto him by the Exorcist, or else he will not give True Answers unto his Demands. But then he tarrieth not one hour in the Truth, unless he be constrained by Divine Power. And his Seal is this, which is to be worn as aforesaid, etc.

NOTES: Text and sigil from the Lesser Key of Solomon, image from the Magus, by Francis Barett.

BELIAL

BELPHEGOR

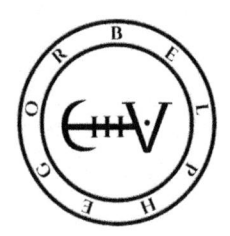

BELPHEGOR, demon of Discoveries and Ingenious inventions. He often takes a young woman's body. He gives riches. The Moabites, who called him Baalphégor, worshipped him on Mount Phégor. Rabbis say that he was paid homage on the pierced chair, and that he was offered the vile residue of digestion. It was worthy of him. That is why some learned see in Belphegor only the god fart or Crepilus; Other scholars argue that it is Priapus. — Selden, quoted by Banier, claims that he was offered human victims, whose priests ate the flesh. Wiérus notes that it is a demon who always has his mouth open; Observing that he must surely belong to the name of Phégor, which means, according to Leloyer, crevasse or split, because he was sometimes worshipped in caves, and that he was thrown offerings through an air hole.

NOTES: Image and text from the Dictionnaire Infernal. Sigil by Arundell Overman.

BELPHEGOR

BERITH

BERITH, Duke in Hell, great and terrible. He is known by three names; Some call him Béal, the Jews call him Bérith and the Necromancers call him Bolfri. He shows himself in the form of a soldier dressed in red from head to toe mounted on a horse of the same color, having a crown on the forehead. He knows the past, the present and the future. He is mastered by the virtue of magic rings; But let's not forget that he is often a liar. He has the talent to change all metals into gold: Also, he is sometimes looked at as the demon of the alchemists. He gives dignity and makes the voice of the singer clear and uplifting. Twenty-six legions are at his command. It was the idol of the Shechemites, and perhaps it is the same as the Béruth of Sanchoniaton that learned believe to be Pallas or Diane. The author of "The solid Treasure of the little Albert" tells of an adventure that would make him believe that this demon is no more than a elf or goblin, if however it is the same Bérith.

"I found myself," said he, "in a castle where a familiar spirit manifested itself, which for six years had taken care to wind the clock and to curry the horses. I was curious one morning to examine this merry-go-round: my astonishment was great to see running the currycomb on the rump of the horse, without it seemed, being driven by any visible hand." The groom told me that in order to attract this leprechaun (or familiar) to his service, he had taken a little black hen, that he had bled her in a great crossroad. Using that blood he had written on a piece of paper: "Bérith will do my work for twenty years, and I shall reward him;" Having then buried the hen at a depth of one foot, the same day the Leprechaun had taken care of the clock and horses. And from time to time it gave the groom things that were worth something...

The historian seems to believe that this imp was a mandrake. The cabalists see no other thing than a sylph.

NOTES: Text and image from the Dictionnaire Infernal, sigil from the Lesser key of Solomon.

BERITH

BIFRONS

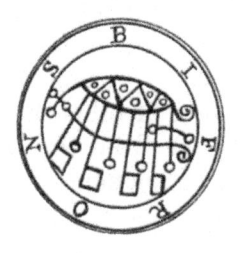

Bifrons, demon that appears with the figure of a monster. When he takes human form, he makes the man learned in astrology, and teaches him to know the influences of the planets; it excels in geometry; He knows the virtues of herbs, gemstones and plants; It transports the corpses from one place to another. He was also seen lighting torches on the tombs of the dead. He has twenty-six legions at his command.

NOTES: Text and image from the Dictionnaire Infernal, sigil from the Lesser key of Solomon.

BIFRONS

BOTIS

BOTIS. The Seventeenth Spirit (of the Lesser Key of Solomon) is Botis, a Great President, and an Earl. He appeareth at the first show in the form of an ugly Viper, then at the command of the Magician he putteth on a Human shape with Great Teeth, and two Horns, carrying a bright and sharp Sword in his hand. He telleth all things Past, and to Come, and reconcileth Friends and Foes. He ruleth over 60 Legions of Spirits, and this is his Seal, etc.

NOTES: Text and sigil from the Lesser key of Solomon. Art created for this book by Matti Sinkkonen.

BOTIS

BRULEFER

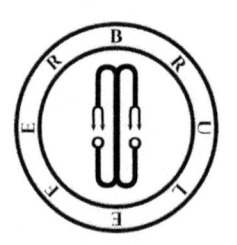

BRULEFER, who causes a person to be beloved of women.

NOTES: Text from the Grimorium Verum. Sigil created by Arundell Overman.

BUCON

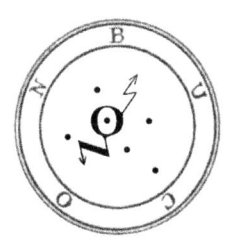

BUCON, can cause hate and spiteful jealousy between members of the opposite sexes.

NOTES: Text from the Grimorium Verum, sigil created by the author.

BUER

BUER, second-class demon, president in the underworld; He has the shape of a star or a wheel with five branches and moves forward rolling on himself. He teaches philosophy, logic and the virtues of medicinal herbs. He boasts of giving good servants and giving health to the sick. He commands fifty legions.

NOTES: Image and text from the Dictionairre Infernal, sigil from the Lesser key of Solomon.

BUER

BUNE

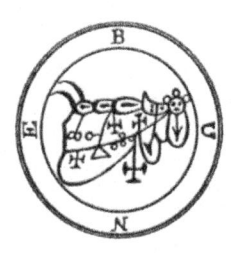

BUNE, or Bime. The Twenty-sixth Spirit (of the Lesser key of Solomon) is Bune (or Bim). He is a Strong, Great and Mighty Duke. He appeareth in the form of a Dragon with three heads, one like a Dog, one like a Gryphon, and one like a Man. He speaketh with a high and comely Voice. He changeth the Place of the Dead, and causeth the Spirits which be under him to gather together upon your Sepulchres. He giveth Riches unto a Man, and maketh him Wise and Eloquent. He giveth true Answers unto Demands. And he governeth 30 Legions of Spirits. His Seal is this, unto the which he oweth Obedience.

NOTES: Text and sigil from the Lesser key of Solomon. Art by Matti Sinkkonen.

BUNE

BYLETH

BYLETH, strong and terrible demon, one of the kings of Hell, according to the Pseudomonarchie of Wierus. He shows himself sitting on a white horse, preceded by cats that sound the horn. The conjurer that evokes it needs a lot of prudence, because it obeys only with fury. It is necessary to submit it to have in hand a stick of coudrier; (a wand of hazel) And, turning to the point that separates the middle of the midday, (southeast) draw outside of the circle, a triangle for the spirit to appear in; Then we read the formula that conjures the spirits, and Byleth arrives in the triangle with submission. If it does not appear, it is because The Exorcist is powerless, and that Hell despises his power. It is also said that when you give Byleth a glass of wine it must be put in the triangle; He obeys more readily and serves the one who treats him. It must be taken care, when it appears, to give him a gracious welcome, to compliment him on his good looks, to show that he and the other kings with him are respected: He's sensitive to all of this. Nor will we neglect, all the time we spend with him, to have at the middle finger of the left hand a ring of silver to be held next to the face. If these conditions are difficult, in reward the one who submits Bylet becomes the most powerful of men. — He was once of the order of the powers; He hopes one day to go back to heaven, to the seventh throne, which is hardly believable. He commands eighty legions.

NOTES: Text and image from the Dictionnaire Infernal, sigil from the Lesser key of Solomon.

BYLETH

CAACRINOLAAS

CAACRINOLAAS, also named Caassimolar and Glassialabolas, great president in the underworld. It comes in the form of a dog, and it has its gait, with Griffon wings. He gives knowledge of the liberal arts, and, by a bizarre contrast, he inspires homicide. It is said that he predicts the future well. This demon makes a man invisible and orders Thirty-six legions. The Grand Grimoire appoints him Classyalabolas, and in fact only a kind of sergeant who sometimes serves as a mount to Nébiros or Naberus.

NOTES: Text and image from the Dictionnaire Infernal, sigil from the Lesser key of Solomon.

CAACRINOLAAS

CAYM

CAYM, upper class demon, great president in the underworld; He usually shows up under the figure of a blackbird. When he appears in human form, he responds from the midst of an ardent blaze; (speaks from within a burning fire) He carries a slender sword in his hand. He is, it is said, the most skillful sophist of hell; And he can, by the trick of his arguments, despair the most seasoned logician. It was with him that Luther had a famous dispute, of which he has spared us the details. Caym gives the understanding of the song of the birds, of the lowing of cattle, the barking of the dogs and the noise of the waves. He knows the future. Sometimes he showed himself as a man wearing a egret headdress and adorned with a peacock's tail. This demon, who was once of the order of the Angels, now commands thirty legions in the underworld.

NOTES: Text and image from the Dictionnaire Infernal, sigil from the Lesser key of Solomon.

CAYM

CERBERUS

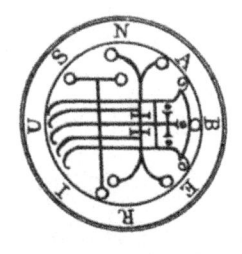

CERBERUS. Cerberus or Naberus is a demon. Wierus puts him among the marquises of the Infernal Empire. He is strong and powerful; He shows himself, when he does not have his three dog heads, in the form of a raven; His voice is hoarse: Nevertheless, he gives eloquence and kindness; He teaches fine arts. Nineteen legions obey him. We see that this is no longer the gatekeeper of the elders, this fearsome dog, incorruptible doorman of the underworld, also called the Beast of the Hundred heads, Centiceps Bellua. Hesiod gives him fifty heads of dog; But one generally agrees to recognize only three. His teeth were black and sharp, and his bite caused a prompt death. It is believed that the fable of Cerberus goes back to the Egyptians, who kept Mastiffs by their tombs. But it was mainly here from the Cerberus demon that we had to deal with. In 1586, he made an alliance with a Picard named Marie Martin.

NOTES: Text and image from the Dictionnaire Infernal, sigil from the Lesser key of Solomon.

CERBERUS

CIMEJES

CIMEJES. The Sixty-sixth Spirit (of the Lesser key of Solomon) is Cimejes, or Cimeies, or Kimaris. He is a Marquis, Mighty, Great, Strong and Powerful, appearing like a Valiant Warrior riding upon a goodly Black Horse. He ruleth over all Spirits in the parts of Africa. His Office is to teach perfectly Grammar, Logic, Rhetoric, and to discover things Lost or Hidden, and Treasures. He governeth 20 Legions of Infernals; and his Seal is this, etc.

NOTES: Text and sigil from the Lesser Key of Solomon. Image drawn for this book by Matti Sinkkonen.

CIMEJES

CLAUNECK

CLAUNECK has power over riches, can cause treasures to be found. He can give great riches to he who makes a pact with him, for he is much loved by Lucifer. It is he who causes money to be brought.

NOTES: Text from the Grimorium Verum, image from the Dictionnaire Infernal, Sigil from the Secrets of Solomon.

CLAUNECK

CLISTHERET

CLISTHERT allows you to have day or night, whichever you wish, when you desire either.

NOTES: Text and sigil from the Grimorium Verum.

CROCELL

CROCELL. The Forty-ninth Spirit (of the Lesser key of Solomon) is Crocell, or Crokel. He appeareth in the Form of an Angel. He is a Duke Great and Strong, speaking something Mystically of Hidden Things. He teacheth the Art of Geometry and the Liberal Sciences. He, at the Command of the Exorcist, will produce Great Noises like the Rushings of many Waters, although there be none. He warmeth Waters, and discovereth Baths. He was of the Order of Potestates, or Powers, before his fall, as he declared unto the King Solomon. He governeth 48 Legions of Spirits. His Seal is this, the which wear thou as aforesaid.

NOTES: Text and sigil from the Lesser Key of Solomon.

CROCELL

DANTALION

DANTALION. The Seventy-first Spirit (of the Lesser key of Solomon) is Dantalion. He is a Duke Great and Mighty, appearing in the Form of a Man with many Countenances, all Men's and Women's Faces; and he hath a Book in his right hand. His Office is to teach all Arts and Sciences unto any; and to declare the Secret Counsel of anyone; for he knoweth the Thoughts of all Men and Women and can change them at his Will. He can cause Love, and show the Similitude of any person, and show the same by a Vision, let them be in what part of the World they Will. He governeth 36 Legions of Spirits; and this is his Seal, which wear thou, etc.

NOTES: Text and Sigil from the Lesser Key of Solomon. Art created for this book by Matti Sinkkonen.

DANTALION

EGIN

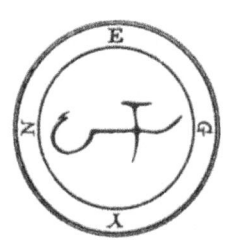

EGIN, king of the North. This spirit is high and mighty. He appeareth in the form of a man with a regal crown, riding upon a dragon: On each side of him are hissing serpents. He cometh with a fearful and tremendous noise, with many inferiors around him, and under him are countless legions of mighty spirits. When constrained by powerful incantations, this spirit assumes the form of a child, and the raising of this spirit is less dangerous than of either of the preceding (kings of the directions) and has proved of great use to the magicians, when rightly invoked. He discovers treasures of the earth and is very tractable.

NOTES: Image and text from "the astrologer of the 19th century." Sigil from the Grimoire known as the "Fasciculus Rerum Geomanticarum."

EGIN

EISHETH ZENUNIM

EISHETH Zenunim. In the Kabbalah, Eisheth Zenunim (Heb. Woman of Whoredom") is a princess of the Qliphoth who rules Sathariel, the order of the Qliphoth of the sphere of Binah, on the tree of death. She is found in the Zohar 1:5a-b as "isheth zennanim" or "qodeshah." In Jewish mythology, she is said to eat the souls of the damned. She is one of the four demon queens along with Lilith, Agrat bat Mahalat, and Naamah. Sigil by the author.

ELELOGAP

ELELOGAP NOTES: Grimorium Verum says he governs matters connected with water, sigil by Arundell Overman. I feel strongly that this spirit is some sort of a mermaid or fish.

EURYNOME

Eurynome, Superior Demon, prince of death, according to some démonomanes. It has large and long teeth, a frightful body all filled with wounds, and for garment a fox skin. The pagans knew him. Pausanias says he feeds on carrion and dead bodies. He had in the Temple of Delphi a statue that represented him with a black complexion, showing his big teeth as a starving wolf and sitting on a vulture's skin.

Notes: Text and image from the Dictionnaire Infernal, Sigil created by Arundell Overman.

EURYNOME

FLAUROS

FLAUROS, Grand General in the underworld. He is seen in the form of a terrible leopard. When he takes the human form, he wears an ugly face, with fiery eyes. He knows the past, the present and the future. He raises all demons or spirits against the enemies of the exorcist and orders twenty legions.

NOTES: Text and image from the Dictionnaire Infernal. Sigil from the Lesser key of Solomon.

FLAUROS

FLEURETY

FLEURETY. The fourth is the Lieutenant General FLERETY, who has the power to perform any task he wishes during the night, he can also cause hail or raise a storm where he wishes. He commands a very considerable corps of spirits, he has under him Bathim, Parsan and Abigar.

NOTES: Text and sigil from the Grand Grimoire, image by Matti Sinkkonen.

FLEURETY

FOCALOR

FOCALOR. The Forty-first Spirit (of the Lesser key of Solomon) is Focalor, or Forcalor, or Furcalor. He is a Mighty Duke and Strong. He appeareth in the Form of a Man with Gryphon's Wings. His office is to slay Men, and to drown them in the Waters, and to overthrow Ships of War, for he hath Power over both Winds and Seas; but he will not hurt any man or thing if he be commanded to the contrary by the Exorcist. He also hath hopes to return to the Seventh Throne after 1,000 years. He governeth 30 Legions of Spirits, and his Seal is this, etc.

NOTES: Text and sigil from the Lesser key of Solomon, art created for this book by Matti Sinkonen.

FOCALOR

FORAS

FORAS. The Thirty-first Spirit (of the Lesser key of Solomon) is Foras. He is a Mighty President, and appeareth in the Form of a Strong Man in Human Shape. He can give the understanding to Men how they may know the Virtues of all Herbs and Precious Stones. He teacheth the Arts of Logic and Ethics in all their parts. If desired he maketh men invisible, and to live long, and to be eloquent. He can discover Treasures and recover things Lost. He ruleth over 29 Legions of Spirits, and his Seal is this, which wear thou, etc.

NOTES: Text and Sigil from the Lesser Key of Solomon, art created for this book by Matti Sinkkonen.

FORAS

FORCAS

FORCAS, or Furcas, knight, great president of the underworld; It appears in the form of a vigorous man, with a long beard and white hair; He is mounted on a large horse and holds a sharp dart. He knows the virtues of the herbs and gemstones. He teaches logic, aesthetics, palmistry, pyromancie and rhetoric. He makes a man invisible, ingenious and handsome. He regains lost things; He discovers treasures, and he has under his orders twenty-nine legions of demons.

NOTES: Image and text from the Dictionnaire Infernal, sigil from the Lesser key of Solomon.

FORCAS

FORNEUS

FORNEUS. The Thirtieth Spirit is Forneus. He is a Mighty and Great Marquis, and appeareth in the Form of a Great Sea-Monster. He teacheth, and maketh men wonderfully knowing in the Art of Rhetoric. He causeth men to have a Good Name, and to have the knowledge and understanding of Tongues. He maketh one to be beloved of his Foes as well as of his Friends. He governeth 29 Legions of Spirits, partly of the Order of Thrones, and partly of that of Angels. His Seal is this, which wear thou, etc.

NOTES: Text and sigil from the Lesser Key of Solomon. Art created for this book by Ville Vuorinen.

FORNEUS

FREYA

FREYA, Norse Goddess of love, sex, and war.

NOTES: Sigil by Arundell Overman, image in the public domain, unknown creator.

FREYA

FRIMOST

FRIMOST has power over women and girls and will help you to obtain their use.

NOTES: Text from the from the Grimorium Verum. Sigil from the Secrets of Solomon.

FRUCISSIERE

FRUCISSIERE revives the dead.

NOTES: Text and sigil from the Grimorium Verum, art created for this book by Ville Vuorinen.

FRUCISSIERE

FRUTIMIERE

Frutimiere prepares all kinds of feasts for you.
Notes: Text and sigil from the Grimorium Verum.

FURFUR

FURFUR, Count in the underworld. He is seen in the form of a deer with a flaming tail; He only tells lies, unless he's locked in a triangle. He often takes the form of an angel, speaks in a hoarse voice and maintains the union between husbands and wives. He makes fall the thunderbolt, the lightning flash, and the thunder groan, in the places he has been ordered to do so. He responds on abstract things. Twenty-six legions are under his command.

NOTES: Text and image from the Dictionnaire Infernal. Sigil from the Lesser key of Solomon.

FURFUR

GOMORY

GOMORY, Mighty Duke of Hell. This demon appears in the form of a beautiful woman; She has a ducal crown on her head, and she rides on a camel. She responds to the present, the past and the future; She discovers hidden treasures, and commands twenty-six legions.

NOTES: Text and image from the Dictionnaire Infernal, sigil from the Lesser key of Solomon.

GOMORY

GULAND

GULAND causes all illnesses.
  NOTES: Text and sigil from the Grimorium Verum.

GUSION

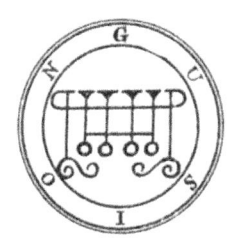

Gusion. The Eleventh Spirit in (the) order (of the Lesser Key of Solomon) is a great and strong Duke, called Gusion. He appeareth like a Xenopilus. He telleth all things, Past, Present, and to Come, and showeth the meaning and resolution of all questions thou mayest ask. He conciliateth and reconcileth friendships, and giveth Honour and Dignity unto any. He ruleth over 40 Legions of Spirits. His Seal is this, the which wear thou as aforesaid.

Notes: Text and sigil from the Lesser Key of Solomon, image public domain, a camel, an unpublished French text known to the author describes him thus.

HAAGENTI

HAAGENTI. The Forty-eighth Spirit (of the Lesser key of Solomon) is Haagenti. He is a President, appearing in the Form of a Mighty Bull with Gryphon's Wings. This is at first, but after, at the Command of the Exorcist he putteth on Human Shape. His Office is to make Men wise, and to instruct them in divers things; also to Transmute all Metals into Gold; and to change Wine into Water, and Water into Wine. He governeth 33 Legions of Spirits, and his Seal is this, etc.

NOTES: Text and sigil from the Lesser key of Solomon.

HAAGENTI

HABORYM

HABORYM, Fire demon, also called Aym. He bears the title of Duke in the underworld. He rides on a viper, and has three heads, one a snake, the other a man, and the third, a cat. He carries a lighted torch in his hand. He commands twenty-six legions.

NOTES: Text and image from the Dictionnaire Infernal, sigil from the Lesser Key of Solomon.

HABORYM

HAEL

HAEL enables anyone to speak in any language he will, and also teaches the means whereby any type of letter may be written. He is also able to teach those things which are most secret and completely hidden.

NOTES: Text and sigil from the Grimorium Verum.

HALAHEL

HALAHEL, a servant of the demon Bael having a mixed nature, partly good, partly evil. Listed in the 1903 Goetia: The Lesser Key of Solomon published by Crowley.

HALPHAS

HALPHAS, or Malthus. The Thirty-eighth Spirit is Halphas, or Malthous (or Malthas). He is a Great Earl, and appeareth in the Form of a Stock-Dove. He speaketh with a hoarse Voice. His Office is to build up Towers, and to furnish them with Ammunition and Weapons, and to send Men-of-War to places appointed. He ruleth over 26 Legions of Spirits, and his Seal is this, etc.

NOTES: Text and sigil from the Lesser Key of Solomon. Picture Source S.G. Goodrich, Animal kingdom illustrated, Volume two, 1859, a pigeon.

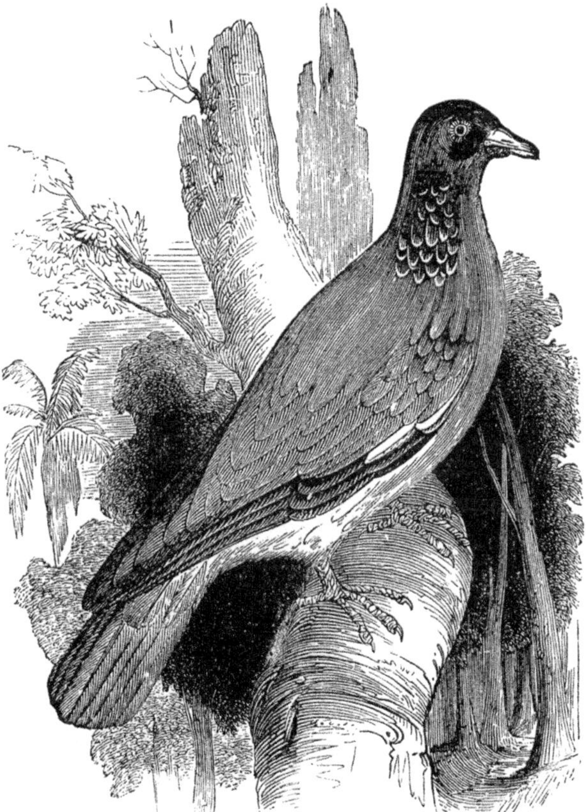

HARISTUM

HARISTUM, who can cause anyone to pass through fire without being touched by it.

NOTES: Text from the Grimorium Verum. Image, public domain, a salamander. Sigil created by Arundell Overman.

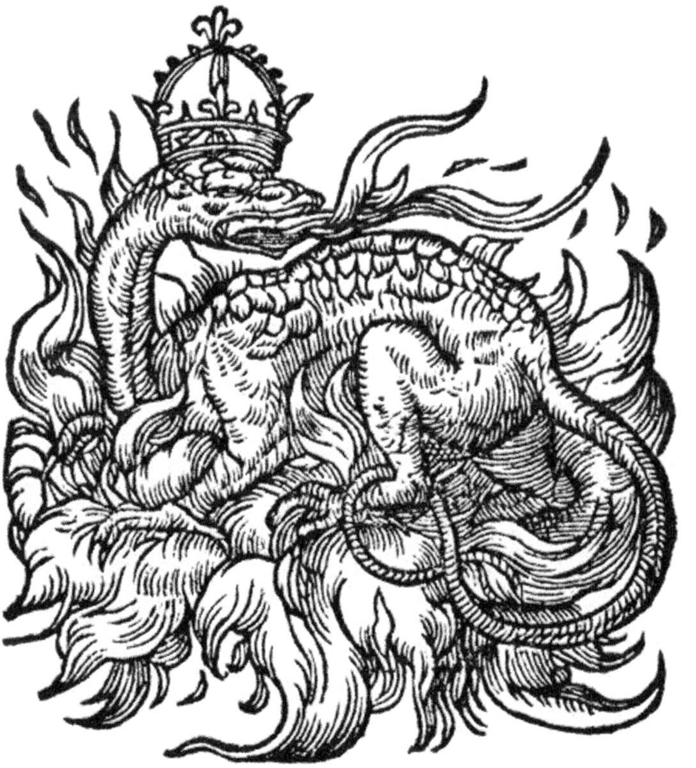

HERAMAEL

HERAMAEL teaches the art of healing, including the complete knowledge of any illness and its cure, He also makes known the virtues of plants, where they are to be found, when to pluck them, and their making into a complete cure.

NOTES: Text and sigil from the Grimorium Verum.

HICPACTH

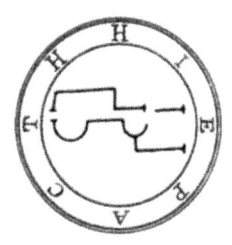

HICPACTH will bring you a person in an instant, though he (or she) be far away.

NOTES: Text and sigil from the Grimorium Verum.

HUICTIIGARAS

HUICTIIGARAS causes sleep in the case of some, and insomnia in others.

NOTES: Text and sigil from the Grimorium Verum. (image, a cat with hypnotic eyes)

HUMOTS

HUMOTS can bring you any book you desire.
NOTES: Text and sigil from the Grimorium Verum, image, public domain, a demon reading a book.

IPÈS

IPÈS or Ayperos, Prince and Earl of Hell; He appears in the form of an angel, sometimes under that of a lion, with the head and paws of a goose and a hare tail, which is a little short. He knows the past and the future, gives of genius and audacity to men, and commands Thirty-six legions.

NOTES: Image and text from the Dictionnaire Infernal, sigil from the Lesser key of Solomon.

IPÈS

KHIL

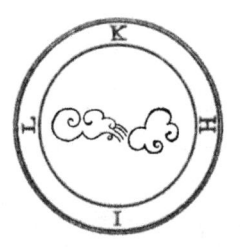

Khil makes great earthquakes.
   Notes: Sigil and text from the GrimoriumVerum.

KLEPOTH

Klepoth makes you see all sorts of dreams and visions.
Notes: Text and sigil from the Grimorium Verum.

LAMASHTU

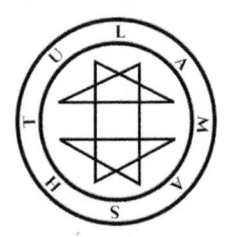

LAMASHTU. In Mesopotamian mythology, Lamashtu was a female demon, monster, malevolent goddess or demigoddess who menaced women during childbirth and, if possible, kidnapped their children while they were breastfeeding. She would gnaw on their bones and suck their blood, as well as being charged with several other evil deeds. She was a daughter of the Sky God Anu.

Lamashtu is depicted as a mythological hybrid, with a hairy body, a lioness' head with donkey's teeth and ears, long fingers and fingernails, and the feet of a bird with sharp talons. She is often shown standing or kneeling on a donkey, nursing a pig and a dog, and holding snakes. She thus bears some functions and resemblance to the Mesopotamian demon Lilith.

Lamashtu's father was the Sky God Anu. Unlike many other usual demonic figures and depictions in Mesopotamian lore, Lamashtu was said to act in malevolence of her own accord, rather than at the gods' instructions. Along with this her name was written together with the cuneiform determinative indicating deity.This means she was a goddess or a demigoddess in her own right.

She bore seven names and was described as seven witches in incantations. Her evil deeds included (but were not limited to): slaying children, and the unborn, causing harm to mothers and expectant mothers; eating men and drinking their blood; disturbing sleep; bringing nightmares; killing foliage; infesting rivers and lakes; and being a bringer of disease, sickness, and death.

Pazuzu, a god or demon, was invoked to protect birthing mothers and infants against Lamashtu's malevolence, usually on amulets and statues. Although Pazuzu was said to be bringer of famine and drought, he was also invoked against evil for protection, and against plague, but he was primarily and popularly invoked against his fierce, malicious rival Lamashtu.

NOTES: Art by Jaeered Serpens. Used with permission.

LAMASHTU

LEONARD

LEONARD, first-order demon, Grand Master of the Sabbaths, leader of the Subordinate Demons, inspector general of witchcraft, black magic and sorcerers. He is often called "le Grand Negre." (the black man) He presides over the Sabbath under the figure of a goat from the waist up. He has three horns on his head, two fox ears, spiky hair, round eyes, inflamed and very open, a goat's beard and a face on his butt. The sorcerers adore him by kissing his lower face with a green candle in their hand. Sometimes he looks like a greyhound or an ox, or a big black bird, or as a tree trunk surmounted by a dark face. His feet, when he attends the Sabbath, are always goose-legged. However, the experts who saw the devil on the Sabbath observe that he has no feet when he takes the form of a tree trunk and in other extraordinary circumstances. Leonard is taciturn and melancholy; But in all the assemblies of wizards and devils where he is obliged to appear, he shows himself advantageously and deploys a superb gravity.

NOTES: Text and image from the Dictionnaire Infernal. Sigil created by Arundell Overman.

LEONARD

LERAJE

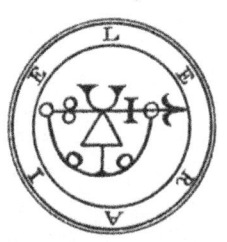

LERAJE, or Leraikha. The Fourteenth Spirit is called Leraje (or Leraie). He is a Marquis Great in Power, showing himself in the likeness of an Archer clad in Green, and carrying a Bow and Quiver. He causeth all great Battles and Contests; and maketh wounds to putrefy that are made with Arrows by Archers. This belongeth unto Sagittary. He governeth 30 Legions of Spirits, and this is his Seal, etc.

NOTES: Text and sigil from the Lesser Key of Solomon, art created for this book by Matti Sinkkonen.

LERAJE

LEVIATHAN

LEVIATHAN is a creature with the form of a sea serpent, referenced in the Hebrew Bible in the Book of Job, Psalms, the Book of Isaiah, and the Book of Amos.

The Leviathan of the Book of Job reflects the older Canaanite Lotan, a primeval monster defeated by the god Baal Hadad. Parallels to the role of Mesopotamian Tiamat defeated by Marduk have long been noted in comparative mythology.

Anton Szandor LaVey in his Satanic Bible (1969) has Leviathan representing the element of Water and the direction of west, listing it as one of the Four Crown Princes of Hell. This association was inspired by the demonic hierarchy from The Book of the Sacred Magic of Abra-Melin the Mage.

NOTES: Sigil from the Grimoire of Armadel, text by Arundell Overman. Art by Gustave Dore.

LEVIATHAN

LILITH

"LILITH—Hebrew female devil, Adam's first wife who taught him the ropes." (A.L.)

Lilith is a figure in Jewish mythology, developed in the Babylonian Talmud , between the 3rd to 5th century AD. Lilith is seen as a dangerous demon of the night, who is sexual, seductive, and steals babies in the darkness. Lilith may be linked in part to a historically earlier class of female demons called lilītu in ancient Mesopotamian religion, found in the cuneiform texts of Sumer, Assyria, and Babylon. In Jewish folklore, from the Alphabet of Ben Sirah in 700–1000 AD onward, Lilith appears as Adam's first wife, before Eve, who was created at the same time and from the same clay as Adam.

The legend of Lilith developed during the Middle Ages, in the Aggadah, and the Zohar, books of Jewish mysticism. In the 13th-century writings of Isaac ben Jacob ha-Cohen, Lilith left Adam after refusing to become submissive to him and "lie beneath" him during sex. She would not return to the Garden of Eden and mated with the archangel/demon Samael, producing demonic children.

Interpretations of Lilith found in Jewish writings are common, but little information has survived relating to the Sumerian, Assyrian, and Babylonian view of this class of demons.

In Hebrew texts, the term lilith or lilit is translated as "night creatures", "night monster", "night hag", or "screech owl". Lilith first appears in the bible, among a list of wild animals in Isaiah 34:14, either in singular or plural form according to variations in the manuscripts. In Jewish magical inscriptions on bowls and amulets from the 6th century AD onward, Lilith is identified as a female demon and the first visual depictions appear. The image of Lilith shown below was created for my books and projects by Anna Levytska, and the text written by me.

LILITH

LUCIFER

Lucifer, the name of the spirit that presides over the orient, according to the opinion of the magicians. Lucifer was evoked on Monday, in a circle in the middle of which was his name. He was content with a mouse as the price for his compliance. He is often taken for the king of the underworld, and according to some démonomanes, he is superior to Satan. It is said that he is sometimes facetious, and that one of his tricks is to remove the brooms on which the witches go to the Sabbath and to give them rides on his shoulders. This is what the Witches of Moira in Sweden attested in 1672. The same witches claimed that they had seen on the Sabbath, the same Lucifer in gray garb, with blue stockings and red pants adorned with ribbons. Lucifer commands the Europeans and Asians. He appears in the form and figure of the most beautiful child. When he is angry, he has a fiery face, but it is nothing monstrous. He is, according to some démonographers, the great vigilante of hell. He is invoked first in the litany of the Sabbath.

NOTES: Text and image from the Dictionnaire Infernal, sigil from the Grimorium Verum.

LUCIFER

LUCIFUGE ROFOCALE

LUCIFUGE Rofocale. The first is the great Lucifuge Rofocale, the infernal Prime Minister who possesses the power that Lucifer gave him over all worldly riches and treasures. He has beneath him Bael, Agares and Marbas along with thousands of other demons or spirits who are his subordinates.

NOTES: Image, text, and sigil from the Grand Grimoire.

LUCIFUGE ROFOCALE

MALPHAS

MALPHAS, great president of the underworld who appears in the form of a raven. When he shows himself with a human figure, the sound of his voice is hoarse; He builds citadels and impregnable towers, overthrows the enemy ramparts, finds good workers, gives familiar spirits, receives sacrifices, and deceives the priests. (those who made sacrifice to him) Forty Legions obey him.

NOTES: Image and text from the Dictionnaire Infernal, sigil from the Lesser key of Solomon.

MALPHAS

MAMMON

MAMMON, demon of avarice: It is he, said Milton, who, first, taught men to tear the bosom of the earth to take out the treasures.

NOTES: Image and text from the Dictionnaire Infernal. Sigil created by Arundell Overman.

MAMMON

MARAX

Marax. The Twenty-first Spirit (of the Lesser Key of Solomon) is Marax. He is a Great Earl and President. He appeareth like a great Bull with a Man's face. His office is to make Men very knowing in Astronomy, and all other Liberal Sciences; also he can give good Familiars, and wise, knowing the virtues of Herbs and Stones which be precious. He governeth 30 Legions of Spirits, and his Seal is this, which must be made and worn as aforesaid, etc.

Notes: Text and Sigil from the Lesser Key of Solomon. Art created for this book by Matti Sinkkonen.

MARAX

MARBAS

MARBAS. The fifth Spirit (of the Lesser Key of Solomon) is Marbas. He is a Great President, and appeareth at first in the form of a Great Lion, but afterwards, at the request of the Master, he putteth on Human Shape. He answereth truly of things Hidden or Secret. He causeth Diseases and cureth them. Again, he giveth great Wisdom and Knowledge in Mechanical Arts; and can change men into other shapes. He governeth 36 Legions of Spirits. And his Seal is this, which is to be worn as aforesaid.

NOTES: Text and Sigil from the Lesser Key of Solomon. Art created by Matti Sinkkonen.

MARBAS

MARCHOCIAS

MARCHOCIAS, Great Marquis of the Underworld. It shows itself in the form of a ferocious female wolf, with wings of a Griffon and a serpent tail: In this graceful form the Marquis vomits flames. When she takes the human form, we think we see a great soldier. she obeys the exorcists, is of the order of domination and commands thirty legions.

NOTES: Text and image from the Dictionnaire Infernal, sigil from the Lesser Key of Solomon.

MARCHOCIAS

MEDUSA

MEDUSA. In Greek mythology, Medusa "guardian, protectress" was a monster, a Gorgon, generally described as a winged human female with living venomous snakes in place of hair. Those who gazed upon her face would turn to stone. Most sources describe her as the daughter of Phorcys and Ceto, though the author Hyginus makes her the daughter of Gorgon and Ceto. According to Hesiod and Aeschylus, she lived and died on an island named Sarpedon, somewhere near Cisthene. The 2nd-century BCE novelist Dionysios Skytobrachion puts her somewhere in Libya, where Herodotus had said the Berbers originated her myth, as part of their religion.

Medusa was beheaded by the hero Perseus, who thereafter used her head, which retained its ability to turn onlookers to stone, as a weapon until he gave it to the goddess Athena to place on her shield. In classical antiquity the image of the head of Medusa appeared in the evil-averting device known as the Gorgoneion.

NOTES: Art created for this book by Anna Levytska. Sigil and text by Arundell Overman.

MEDUSA

MERSILDE

MERSILDE has the power to transport anyone in an instant, anywhere.

NOTES: Text and Sigil from the Grimorium Verum.

MINOSON

MINOSON, is able to make anyone win at any game.

NOTES: Text from the Grimorium Verum. Image public domain, a court jester. Sigil by the author.

MOLOCH

MOLOCH, Prince of the Land of tears, member of the Infernal Council. He was worshipped by the Ammonites under the figure of a bronze statue seated in a throne of the same metal, with a calf's head surmounted by a royal crown. His arms were extended to receive human victims: they were sacrificed children. In Milton, Moloch is an awful and terrible demon covered with the cries of mothers, and children's blood. The rabbis claim that in the interior of the statue of the famous Moloch, god of the Ammonites, seven kinds of cabinets had been arranged. One opened for the flour, another for the doves, a third for a sheep, a fourth for a ram, the fifth for a calf, the sixth for an ox, the seventh for a child. This gave rise to the confusing of Moloch with Mithra, and his seven mysterious gates with the seven chambers. When one wanted to sacrifice children to Moloch, a great fire was lit in the interior of this statue. But in order not to hear their plaintive cries, the priests made a great sound of drums and other instruments around the idol.

NOTES: Image and text from the Dictionnaire Infernal, sigil created by Arundell Overman.

MOLOCH

MORAIL

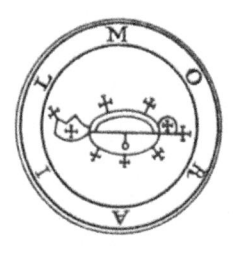

Morail can make anything invisible.
NOTES: Text and sigil from the Grimorium Verum.

MURMUR

MURMUR, or Murmus. The Fifty-fourth Spirit (in the Lesser Key of Solomon) is called Murmur, or Murmus, or Murmux. He is a Great Duke, and an Earl; and appeareth in the Form of a Warrior riding upon a. Gryphon, with a Ducal Crown upon his Head. There do go before him those his Ministers, with great Trumpets sounding. His Office is to teach Philosophy perfectly, and to constrain Souls Deceased to come before the Exorcist to answer those questions which he may wish to put to them, if desired. He was partly of the Order of Thrones, and partly of that of Angels. He now ruleth 30 Legions of Spirits. And his Seal is this, etc.

NOTES: Text and sigil from the Lesser Key of Solomon.

MURMUR

MUSISIN

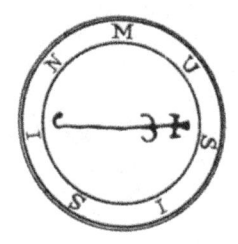

MUSISIN has power over great lords, teaches all that happens in the Republics, and the affairs of the Allies.

NOTES: Text from the Grimorium Verum

NAAMAH

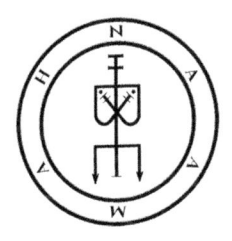

NAAMAH or Na'amah (Hebrew: "pleasant") is a demon described in the Zohar, a foundational work of Jewish mysticism. She is often conflated with another Naamah, sister to Tubal-cain. According to the Zohar, after Cain kills Abel, Adam separates from Eve for 130 years. During this time, Lilith and Naamah visit him and bear his demonic children, who became the Plagues of Mankind. She and Lilith cause epilepsy in children. Naamah is considered one of the mates of the archangel Samael along with Lilith and Agrat bat Mahlat, sometimes also adding Eisheth. In another story from the Zohar, Naamah is said to have corrupted Samyaza/Ouza and Azael. Other versions have both Naamah and Lilith at it.

NOTES: Text and sigil by Arundell Overman.

NAIN-LAURIN

NAIN-LAURIN or the Elf-king. It is the king of small Elfs, kobolds and other dwarf spirits. Kobold, spirit of the class of the elves. "It is a strange little dwarf, of stunted form, with motley clothes, a red bonnet on his head. Honored by the valets, the servants and the cooks of Germany, he makes them good offices-he currycombs their horses, he washes the house, keeps the kitchen in good order and watches over everything so that we don't think about neglecting it."

NOTES: Text and image from the Dictionnaire Infernal. Sigil created by Arundell Overman.

NAIN-LAURIN

NEBIROS

NEBIROS. The sixth Superior Spirit is NEBIROS, Camp Marshal and Inspector General, who has the power to harm whoever he pleases, he can reveal the Hand of Glory, he educates on all the qualities of Metals, Minerals, Plants and all pure & impure Animals. He also grants the art of predicting the future, being one of the greatest necromancers of all the infernal spirits. He can go anywhere and inspect all the infernal militias. He has under him Ayperos, Nuberus and Glasyabolas

NOTES: Text from the Grand Grimoire, Sigil from the Grimorium Verum. Art created for this book by Ville Vuorinen.

NIBIROS

NICKAR

NICKAR or Nick. According to Scandinavian mythology, the main source of all beliefs popular in Germany and England, Odin takes the name of Nickar or Hnickar when he acts as a destructive or evil genius. Under this name and in the form of kelpie, the horse-devil of Scotland, he lives in the lakes and rivers of Scandinavia, where he raises storms and hurricanes. There is a dark lake with murky waters and thick, wood-covered shores, in which lies the island of Rugen. This is where he likes to torment sinners by capsizing their boats and sometimes throwing them to the top of the highest fir trees. From the Scandinavian Nickar came the water men and the water women, the nixies of the Teutons. There is no more famous than the nymphs of the Elbe and Gaal. Prior to the establishment of Christianity, the Saxons who lived in the vicinity of these two rivers worshipped a female deity, whose temple was in the city of Magdeburg or Megdeburch (city of the girl), and which always inspired for some, fear, as the Naiad of the Elbe. She appeared in Magdeburg, where she was accustomed to go to the market with a basket under her arm: She was full of grace, clean, and at first sight, would have been taken for the daughter of a good bourgeois; But the malignant recognized her, by a small corner of her apron, always wet, in memory of her aquatic origin. In the English, the sailors call the devil, the Old Nick.

NOTES: Text and image from the Dictionnaire Infernal. Sigil created by Arundell Overman.

NICKAR

ORIAX

ORIAX, or Orias. The Fifty-ninth Spirit (of the Lesser Key of Solomon) is Oriax, or Orias. He is a Great Marquis, and appeareth in the Form of a Lion,26 riding upon a Horse Mighty and Strong, with a Serpent's Tail; and he holdeth in his Right Hand two Great Serpents hissing. His Office is to teach the Virtues of the Stars, and to know the Mansions of the Planets, and how to understand their Virtues. He also transformeth Men, and he giveth Dignities, Prelacies, and Confirmation thereof; also Favour with Friends and with Foes. He doth govern 30 Legions of Spirits; and his Seal is this, etc.

NOTES: Text and Sigil from the Lesser Key of Solomon.

ORIAX

ORIENS

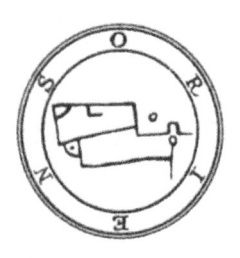

ORIENS. King of the East. He appeareth with a fair and feminine countenance, and a goodly crown upon his head; he rideth upon an elephant, having before him numbers of musical instruments. Sometimes he appeareth in the similitude of a horse; and, when he is constrained by magical incantations, assumeth a human shape. He hath under him 250 legions of inferior spirits. His power, according to the ancients, is great, and he can answer truly of all demands, both past, present and to come.

NOTES: Image and text from "The astrologer of the 19th century." Sigil from the Grimoire "Fasciculus Rerum Geomanticarum."

ORIENS

OROBAS

OROBAS, great Prince of the Dark Empire. He is seen in the form of a beautiful horse. When he appears under the figure of a man, he speaks of the divine essence. Consulted, it gives answers about the past, the present and the future. He discovers falsehood, bestows dignity and jobs, reconciles enemies, and has under his command twenty legions.

NOTES: Text and Image from the Dictionnaire Infernal, sigil from the Lesser Key of Solomon.

OROBAS

OSE

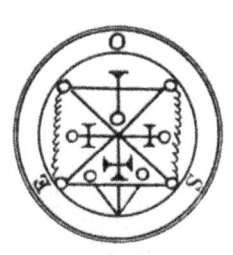

OSE, or Voso. The Fifty-seventh Spirit (of the Lesser Key of Solomon) is Oso, Ose, or Voso. He is a Great President, and appeareth like a Leopard at the first, but after a little time he putteth on the Shape of a Man. His Office is to make one cunning in the Liberal Sciences, and to give True Answers of Divine and Secret Things; also to change a Man into any Shape that the Exorcist pleaseth, so that he that is so changed will not think any other thing than that he is in verity that Creature or Thing he is changed into. He governeth 30 Legions of Spirits, and this is his Seal, etc.

NOTES: Text and sigil from the Lesser Key of Solomon.

OSE

PAPA LEGBA

Papa Legba, African god, spirit of the crossroads. Papa Legba is a loa in Haitian Vodou, who serves as the intermediary between the loa and humanity. He stands at a spiritual crossroads and gives (or denies) permission to speak with the spirits of Guinee, in Vodou, Guinee is the spirit world. It is where the souls of the dead live and is believed to speak all human languages. In Haiti, he is the great elocutioner, or master public speaker. Legba facilitates communication, speech, and understanding. He is commonly associated with dogs. He usually appears as an old man on a crutch or with a cane, wearing a broad brimmed straw hat and smoking a pipe. The dog is sacred to him. Legba is syncretized with Saint Peter, Saint Lazarus, and Saint Anthony.

In Benin, Nigeria and Togo, Legba is viewed as young and virile trickster deity, often horned and phallic, and his shrine is usually located at the gate of the village in the countryside. Alternatively, he is addressed as Legba Atibon, Atibon Legba, or Ati-Gbon Legba.

Notes: Text by Arundell Overman, sigil created from the traditional symbol of the god.

PAZUZU

PAZAZU In ancient Mesopotamian religion, Pazuzu was the king of the demons of the wind, brother of Humbaba and son of the god Hanbi. He also represented the southwestern wind, the bearer of storms and drought. Pazuzu is often depicted as a combination of diverse animal and human parts. He has the body of a man, the head of a lion or dog, talons of an eagle, two pairs of wings, and a scorpion's tail. He has his right hand up and left hand down.

Pazuzu is the demon of the southwest wind known for bringing famine during dry seasons, and locusts during rainy seasons. Pazuzu was invoked in apotropaic amulets, which combat the powers of his rival, the malicious goddess Lamashtu, who was believed to cause harm to mother and child during childbirth. Although Pazuzu is, himself, considered to be an evil spirit, he drives and frightens away other evil spirits, therefore protecting humans against plagues and misfortunes.

NOTES: Text and sigil by Arundell Overman.

PAYMON

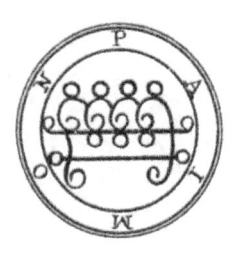

PAYMON, one of the Kings of Hell. If he shows himself to the exorcists, it is in the form of a man riding on a camel, crowned with a glittering jewel encircled tiara, with a woman's face. Two hundred legions, part of the Order of the Angels, part of the order of the powers, obey him. If Paymon is evoked by a sacrifice or libation, he appears accompanied by the two great Princes Bébal and Abalam. NOTES; Text and image from the Dictionnaire Infernal, sigil from the Lesser Key of Solomon. The "astrologer of the 19th century" notes..." Paymon, king of the West. This spirit is powerful to evil, appearing in the likeness of an armed soldier, riding upon a camel or dromedary, being crowned with a bright crown: his countenance is feminine, but his voice hoarse and uncouth. Before him goeth all kinds of musical instruments: yet, when constrained by art, he readily performs the desired wishes of the invocator, and hath under him an infinity of spirits."

PAYMON

PENTAGNONY

PENTAGNONY, who gives the two benefits of attaining invisibility and the love of great lords.

NOTES: Text from the Grimorium Verum, sigil created by Arundell Overman.

PHENEX

PHENEX. The Thirty-Seventh Spirit (of the Lesser Key of Solomon) is Phenex (or Pheynix). He is a great Marquis, and appeareth like the Bird Phoenix, having the Voice of a Child. He singeth many sweet notes before the Exorcist, which he must not regard, but by-and-by he must bid him put on Human Shape. Then he will speak marvellously of all wonderful Sciences if required. He is a Poet, good and excellent. And he will be willing to perform thy requests. He hath hopes also to return to the Seventh Throne after 1,200 years more, as he said unto Solomon. He governeth 20 Legions of Spirits. And his Seal is this, which wear thou, etc.

NOTES: Text and sigil from the Lesser Key of Solomon.

PHENEX

PROCULO

PROCULO, who can cause a person to sleep for forty-eight hours, with the knowledge of the spheres of sleep.

NOTES: Text from the Grimorium Verum, sigil by Arundell Overman.

PRUSLAS

PRUSLAS or Pruflas otherwise found as Bufas, is a great prince and duke, whose abode is around the Tower of Babylon, and there he is seen like a flame outside. His head however is like that of a great night hawk. He is the author and promoter of discord, war, quarrels, and falsehood. He may not be admitted into every place. He responds generously to your requests. Under him are twenty-six legions, partly of the order of Thrones, and partly of the order of Angels.

NOTES: Text from the Dictionnaire Infernal, sigil by Frater V.I.M., and in the public domain. Image created for this book by Ville Vuorinen.

PURSAN

PURSAN or Curson, great king of Hell. He appears in the human form, with a head reminiscent of the lion; He holds a snake; He is mounted on a bear and continually preceded by the sound of the trumpet. He knows deeply the present, the past, and the future, and discovers things buried, like treasures. Taking the form of a man, his body is aerial; He is the giver of good familiar spirits. Twenty-two legions receive his orders.

NOTES: Text and image from the Dictionnaire Infernal, sigil from the Lesser Key of Solomon.

PURSAN

RAUM

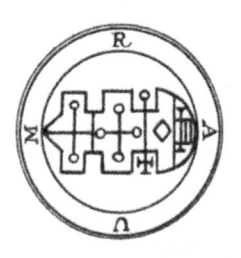

RAUM. The Fortieth Spirit (of the Lesser Key of Solomon) is Raum. He is a Great Earl; and appeareth at first in the Form of a Crow, but after the Command of the Exorcist he putteth on Human Shape. His office is to steal Treasures out King's Houses, and to carry it whither he is commanded, and to destroy Cities and Dignities of Men, and to tell all things, Past and What Is, and what Will Be; and to cause Love between Friends and Foes. He was of the Order of Thrones. He governeth 30 Legions of Spirits; and his Seal is this, which wear thou as aforesaid.

NOTES: Text and sigil from the Lesser Key of Solomon. Image public domain, a crow.

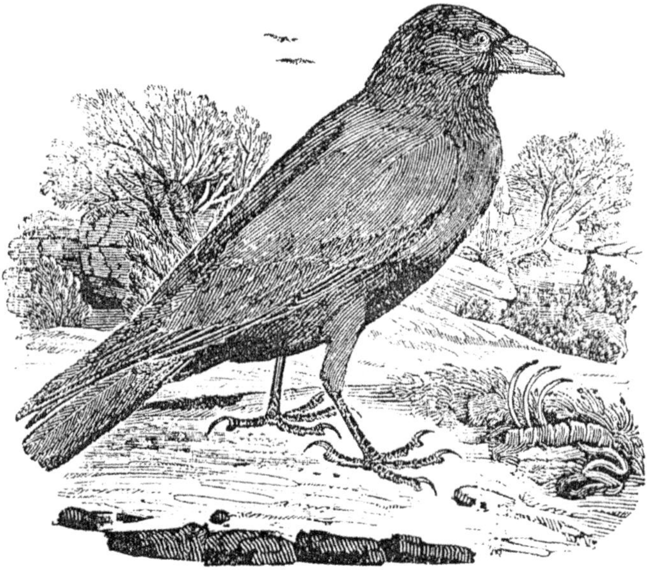

RONWE

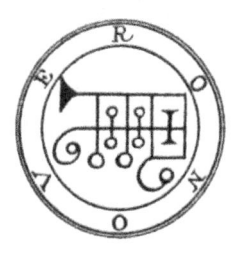

RONWE, Marquis and Count of Hell, who appears in the form of a monster; It gives its followers the knowledge of languages and the well-being of everyone. Nineteen infernal legions are under his command.

NOTES: Text and image from the Dictionnaire Infernal, sigil from the Lesser Key of Solomon.

RONWE

SABNOCK

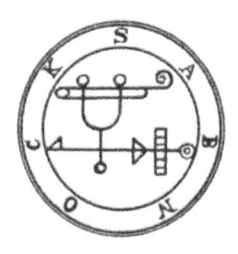

SABNOCK. The Forty-third Spirit, as King Solomon commanded them into the Vessel of Brass, (in the Lesser Key) is called Sabnock, or Savnok. He is a Marquis, Mighty, Great and Strong, appearing in the Form of an Armed Soldier with a Lion's Head, riding on a pale-coloured horse. His office is to build high Towers, Castles and Cities, and to furnish them with Armour, etc. Also he can afflict Men for many days with Wounds and with Sores rotten and full of Worms. He giveth Good Familiars at the request of the Exorcist. He commandeth 50 Legions of Spirits; and his Seal is this.

NOTES: Text and sigil from the Lesser Key of Solomon.

SABNOCK

SAMAGINA

SAMIGINA, or Gamigin. The Fourth Spirit (of the Lesser Key of Solomon) is Samigina, a Great Marquis. He appeareth in the form of a little Horse or Ass, and then into Human shape doth he change himself at the request of the Master. He speaketh with a hoarse voice. He ruleth over 30 Legions of Inferiors. He teaches all Liberal Sciences, and giveth account of Dead Souls that died in sin. And his Seal is this, which is to be worn before the Magician when he is Invocator, etc.

NOTES: Text and sigil from the Lesser Key of Solomon, image public domain, a donkey.

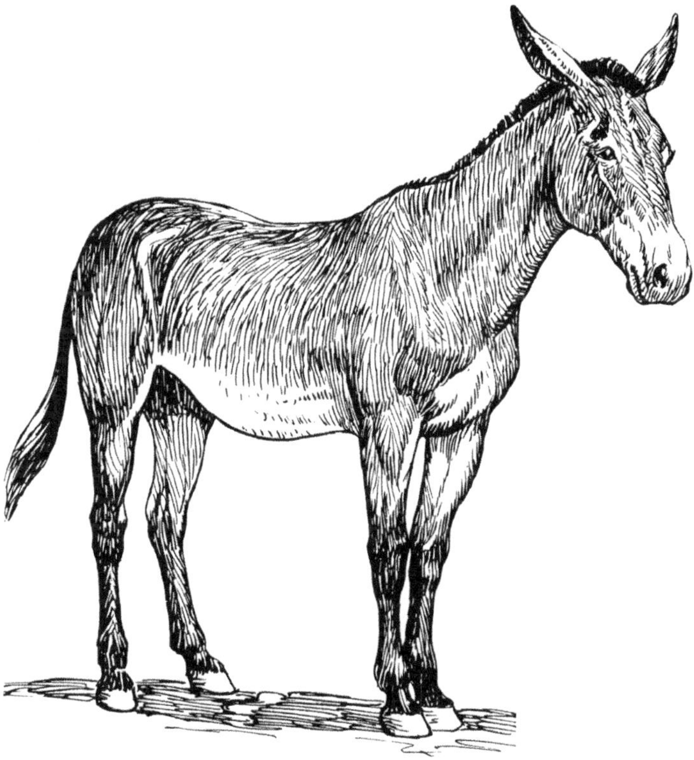

SARGATANAS

SARGATANAS. The fifth (spirit under the three ruling chiefs) is Brigadier Sargatanas, who has the power to make one invisible, to transport one anywhere, to open all locks, to grant one the power to see whatever is happening inside homes, to teach all the tricks and subtleties of the Shepherds. He controls several brigades of spirits. He has under him Loray, Valefar and Farau.

NOTES: Text from the Grand Grimoire, sigil from the Grimorium Verum, art created for this book by Ville Vuorinen.

SARGATANAS

SATANACHIA

SATANACHIA. He has power over women and girls. He also has the power to make a person young or old.

NOTES: Sigil and text from the Grand Grimoire, Image created for this book by Ville Vuorinen.

SATANACHIA

SCIRLIN

SCIRLIN. This spirit acts as an intermediary between the magician and other spirits and can go and get them for you. Contact this spirit first, and he can bring you any other spirit.

NOTES: Source, Grimorium Verum.

SCOX

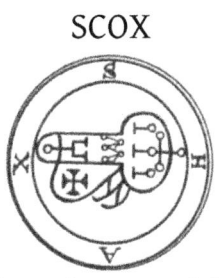

SCOX or Chax, Duke and Grand Marquis of the Underworld. He has a hoarse voice, a Spirit who lies; It comes in the form of a stork. He steals money from the houses that own it and returns it only after twelve hundred years. He carries the horses off. He executes all the commandments which he is given when required to act immediately; And even though he promises to obey the exorcists, he doesn't always do it. He lies, if he is not in a triangle; If on the contrary he is confined in the triangle, he speaks the truth by talking about supernatural things. He indicates hidden treasures that are not guarded by evil spirits. He commands thirty legions.

NOTES: Text and image from the Dictionnaire Infernal, sigil from the Lesser Key of Solomon.

SEERE

SEERE, Sear, or Seir. The Seventieth Spirit (of the Lesser Key of Solomon) is Seere, Sear, or Seir. He is a Mighty Prince, and Powerful, under Amaymon, King of the East. He appeareth in the Form of a Beautiful Man, riding upon a Winged Horse. His Office is to go and come; and to bring abundance of things to pass on a sudden, and to carry or recarry anything whither thou wouldest have it to go, or whence thou wouldest have it from. He can pass over the whole Earth in the twinkling of an Eye. He giveth a True relation of all sorts of Theft, and of Treasure hid, and of many other things. He is of an indifferent Good Nature and is willing to do anything which the Exorcist desireth. He governeth 26 Legions of Spirits. And this his Seal is to be worn, etc.

NOTES: Text, and sigil from the Lesser Key of Solomon. Image created for this book by Matti Sinkkonen.

SEERE

SEGAL

SEGAL will cause all sorts of prodigies to appear.

NOTES: Text and sigil from the Grimorium Verum. Prodigy, meaning an amazing or unusual thing, especially one out of the ordinary course of nature.

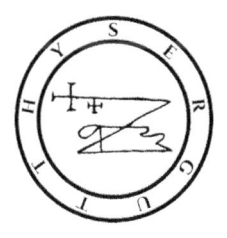

SERGUTTHY

SERGUTTHY has power over maidens and wives, when things are favorable.

NOTES: Text and sigil from the Grimorium Verum.

SIDRAGOSAM

SIDRAGOSAM, causes any girl to dance in the nude.
NOTES: Text from the Grimorium Verum, sigil by Arundell Overman, art created for this book by Ville Vuorinen.

SIDRAGOSAM

SIRCHARDE

SIRCHADE makes you see all sorts of natural and supernatural animals.

NOTES: Text and sigil from the Grimorium Verum, image public domain, a chimera.

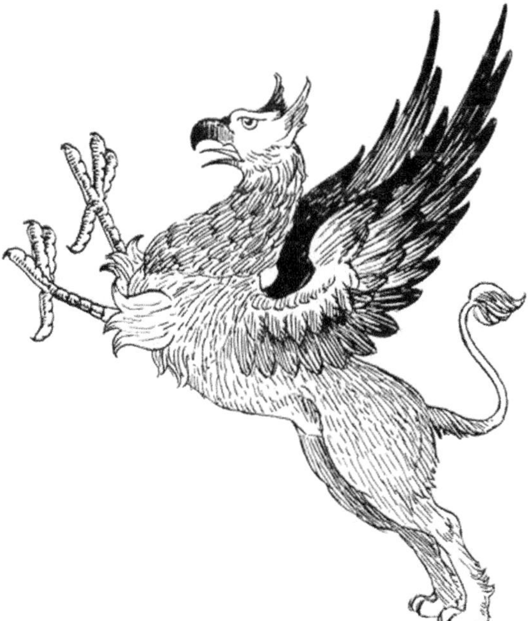

SITRI

SITRI. The Twelfth Spirit (of the Lesser Key of Solomon) is Sitri. He is a Great Prince and appeareth at first with a Leopard's head and the Wings of a Gryphon, but after the command of the Master of the Exorcism he putteth on Human shape, and that very beautiful. He enflameth men with Women's love, and Women with Men's love; and causeth them also to show themselves naked if it be desired. He governeth 60 Legions of Spirits. His Seal is this, to be worn as a Lamen before thee, etc.

NOTES: Text and sigil from the Lesser Key of Solomon.

SITRI

STOLAS

STOLAS, great Prince of the underworld, who appears in the form of an owl. When he takes that of a man and shows himself before The Exorcist, he teaches astronomy, as well as the properties of plants and the value of precious stones. Twenty-six legions recognize him for a general.

NOTES: Text and image from the Dictionnaire Infernal. Sigil from the Lesser Key of Solomon.

STOLAS

SURGAT

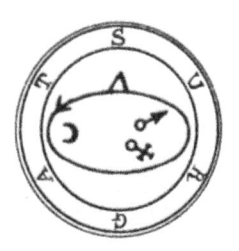

Surgat opens every kind of lock.

Notes: Text from the Grimorium Verum, sigil from the Grimoire of Honorius.

SUSTUGRIEL

SUSTUGRIEL teaches the art of magic. He gives familiar spirits that can be used for all purposes, and he also gives mandragores.

NOTES: Text and sigil from the Grimorium Verum.

SYBILIA

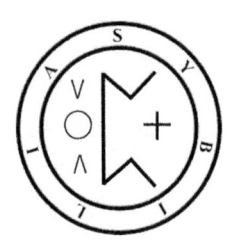

SYBILIA is a fairy described in the 16th century text "The Discovery of Witchcraft" by Reginald Scott. She has two fairy sisters, named Mylia, and Achilia, and she grants Invisibility, and if the is pleased with the one who calls her up, she may have "carnal copulation" with them.

NOTES: Sigil and text by Arundell Overman.

SYRACH

DUKE SYRACH. Grimorium Verum says he is the commander of the following 18 spirits.

I. Clauneck
II. Musisin
III. Bechaud
IV. Frimost
V. Klepoth
VI. Khil
VII. Mersilde
VIII. Clisthert
IX. Sirchade
X. Segal
XI. Hicpacth
XII. Humots
XIII. Frucissiere
XIV. Guland
XV. Surgat
XVI. Morail
XVII. Frutimiere
XVIII. Huictiigaras

TAP

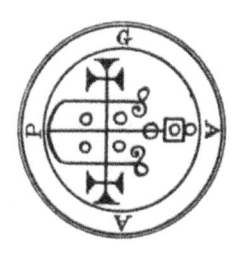

TAP or Gaap, great president and Great Prince in the underworld. He shows up at noon when he takes the human form. He commands four of the main kings of the Infernal Empire. He's as powerful as Byleth. There were once necromancers who offered him libations and holocausts; They evoked him by means of magic tricks which they said were composed by the very wise King Solomon; Which is untrue, for it was Cham, son of Noah, who first began to conjure up evil spirits. He was made to serve Byleth and composed an art in his name, and a book that is appreciated by many mathematicians. Another book is quoted from the Prophets Elijah and Elisha, by which we conjure Gaap under the holy Names of God contained in the keys of Solomon. If any exorcist knows the art of Byleth, GAAP or Tap will not be able to withstand the presence of the Exorcist. Gaap or Tap excites to love, or to hatred. He has an empire over the demons subjected to the power of Amaymon. He transports men very quickly in the different regions they want to travel. He commands sixty legions.

NOTES: Image and text from the Dictionnaire Infernal, sigil from the Lesser Key of Solomon.

TAP

TRIMASAEL

Trimasael teaches chemistry and all means of conjuring of the nature of deceit or sleight-of hand. He also teaches the secret of making the Powder of Projection, by means of which the base metals may be turned into gold or silver.

Notes: Text and sigil from the Grimorium Verum.

VALEFOR

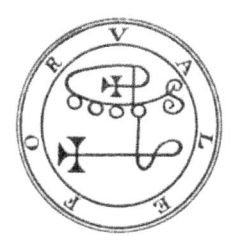

VALEFOR. The Sixth Spirit (of the Lesser Key of Solomon) is Valefor. He is a mighty Duke, and appeareth in the shape of a Lion with an Ass's Head, bellowing. He is a good Familiar, but tempteth them he is a familiar of to steal. He governeth 10 Legions of Spirits. His Seal is this, which is to be worn, whether thou wilt have him for a Familiar or not.

NOTES: Text and sigil from the Lesser Key of Solomon, image created for this book by Ville Vuorinen.

VALEFOR

VAPULA

VAPULA, or Naphula. The Sixtieth Spirit (of the Lesser Key of Solomon) is Vapula, or Naphula. He is a Duke Great, Mighty, and Strong; appearing in the Form of a. Lion with Gryphon's Wings. His Office is to make Men Knowing in all Handcrafts and Professions, also in Philosophy, and other Sciences. He governeth 36 Legions of Spirits, and his Seal or Character is thus made, and thou shalt wear it as aforesaid, etc.

NOTES: Text and sigil from the Lesser key of Solomon.

VAPULA

VASSAGO

Vassago. The Third Spirit (of the Lesser Key of Solomon) is a Mighty Prince, being of the same nature as Agares. He is called Vassago. This Spirit is of a Good Nature, and his office is to declare things Past and to Come, and to discover all things Hid or Lost. And he governeth 26 Legions of Spirits, and this is his Seal.

NOTES: Text and sigil from the Lesser Key of Solomon. Art created for this book by Matti Sinkkonen.

VASSAGO

VEPAR

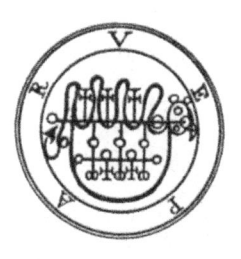

VEPAR. The Forty-second Spirit (of the Lesser Key of Solomon) is Vepar, or Vephar. He is a Duke Great and Strong and appeareth like a Mermaid. His office is to govern the Waters, and to guide Ships laden with Arms, Armour, and Ammunition, etc., thereon. And at the request of the Exorcist he can cause the seas to be right stormy and to appear full of ships. Also he maketh men to die in Three Days by Putrefying Wounds or Sores, and causing Worms to breed in them. He governeth 29 Legions of Spirits, and his Seal is this, etc.

NOTES: Text and sigil from the Lesser Key of Solomon.

VEPAR

VINE

VINE. The Forty-fifth Spirit (of the Lesser Key of Solomon) is Vine, or Vinea. He is a Great King, and an Earl; and appeareth in the Form of a Lion, riding upon a Black Horse, and bearing a Viper in his hand. His Office is to discover Things Hidden, Witches, Wizards, and Things Present, Past, and to Come. He, at the command of the Exorcist will build Towers, overthrow Great Stone Walls, and make the Waters rough with Storms. He governeth 36 Legions of Spirits. And his Seal is this, which wear thou, as aforesaid, etc.

NOTES: Text and sigil from the Lesser Key of Solomon.

VINE

VOLAC

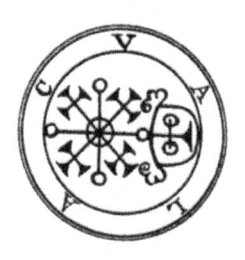

VOLAC, great president in the underworld; He appears in the form of a child with wings of an angel, mounted on a two-headed dragon. He knows the position of the planets and the hiding places of the serpents. Thirty legions obey Him.

NOTES: Text and image from the Dictionnaire Infernal, sigil from the Lesser Key of Solomon.

VOLAC

WALL

WALL, great and mighty Duke of the Dark Empire; It has the shape of a high and terrible dromedary; If he takes a human figure, he speaks Egyptian; He knows the present, the past and the future. He was of the order of the powers. Thirty-six Legions are under his command.

NOTES: Text and Image from the Dictionnaire Infernal, sigil from the Lesser Key of Solomon.

WALL

ZAEBOS

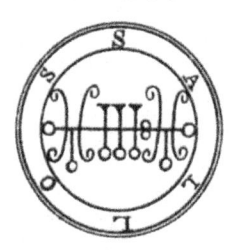

ZAEBOS, great Count of the underworld. He has the figure of a handsome soldier mounted on a crocodile; His head is adorned with a ducal crown. He is sweet of character.

NOTES: Text and image from the Dictionnaire Infernal, sigil from the Lesser Key of Solomon.

ZAEBOS

ZAGAN

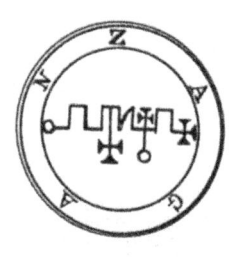

ZAGAN. The Sixty-first Spirit (of the Lesser Key of Solomon) is Zagan. He is a Great King and President, appearing at first in the Form of a Bull with Gryphon's Wings; but after a while he putteth on Human Shape. He maketh Men Witty. He can turn Wine into Water, and Blood into Wine, also Water into Wine. He can turn all Metals into Coin of the Dominion that Metal is of. He can even make Fools wise. He governeth 33 Legions of Spirits, and his Seal is this, etc.

NOTES: Text and sigil from the Lesser Key of Solomon. Art by Matti Sinkkonen.

ZAGAN

ZEPAR

ZEPAR. The Sixteenth Spirit (of the Lesser Key of Solomon) is Zepar. He is a Great Duke, and appeareth in Red Apparel and Armour, like a Soldier. His office is to cause Women to love Men, and to bring them together in love. He also maketh them barren. He governeth 26 Legions of Inferior Spirits, and his Seal is this, which he obeyeth when he seeth it.

NOTES: Text and sigil from the Lesser Key of Solomon.

ZEPAR

Printed in Great Britain
by Amazon